Keto Dinner Recipes

50 Easy Made Keto Dinner Recipes

Table of Contents

INTRODUCTION 4

KETO CHICKEN DIANE 5

CREAMY LEMON ARTICHOKE CHICKEN 7

SPAGHETTI SQUASH CACIO E PEPE 9

KETO CREAMY CHICKEN PICCATA 11

LOADED BELL PEPPER NACHOS 13

KETO BEEF STROGANOFF 15

RANCH CHICKEN MEATBALLS 17

KETO PORK PICCATA 19

CHIPOTLE CHEDDAR CAULIFLOWER "MAC AND CHEESE" 21

KETO MEXICAN BEEF BOWLS 23

KETO MAPLE WALNUT SALMON 25

PIZZA BIANCA (WHITE PIZZA) WITH SUN-DRIED TOMATOES AND BROCCOLI 27

KETO MAC AND CHEESE WITH ZOODLES 29

SMOKED SALMON EGG POTS 31

GLUTEN-FREE, LOW CARB & KETO FISH AND CHIPS 33

LOW CARB CHICKEN AND CAULIFLOWER LASAGNE 35

LOW-CARB PALMINI CARBONARA WITH KALE AND SAUSAGES 37

LOW-CARB MOUSSAKA 39

ONE-PAN PARMESAN CHICKEN DINNER 41

HERBED BUTTER WHOLE ROASTED CHICKEN 43

BAKED CHICKEN WITH POTATOES & ONIONS 45

CHICKEN VEGGIE PACKETS 47

ROASTED SHRIMP AND GREEN BEANS 49

BRUSSELS SPROUTS WITH APPLES AND BACON 51

KETO BOK CHOY - GINGER STIR-FRY 53

CHICKEN ENCHILADA SKILLET 55

KETO CRAB ALFREDO 57

BAKED - CREAMY BEEF NOODLE 59

KETO ZUCCHINI RAVIOLI 61

PROSCIUTTO-WRAPPED CHICKEN WITH MUSHROOM SAUCE 63

MACADAMIA-CRUSTED FISH WITH HERB SALAD	65
MAPLE-GLAZED SALMON WITH SPINACH AND BROCCOLINI	67
LOW CARB MOROCCAN LAMB WITH CARROT	69
PLUM AND SMOKED TROUT SCANDI BOWL	71
KETO PRAWN TOM YUM	73
CHILI-LIME BAKED SALMON IN FOIL	75
EASY KETO BAKED ITALIAN SAUSAGE	77
KETO COD PICCATA	79
KETO BLACKENED HALIBUT	81
KETO CHICKEN FLORENTINE	83
KETO CAJUN SHRIMP AND GRITS	85
HERBED GORGONZOLA STEAK BUTTER	87
GARLIC BUTTER STEAK BITES WITH CAULIFLOWER	89
CHEESY BUFFALO CAULIFLOWER DISH	91
TURKEY CUTLETS WITH ROSEMARY AND THYME	93
KETO PUMPKIN CHILI	95
KETO CAJUN JAMBALAYA	97
GARLIC BUTTER INSTANT POT SHORT RIBS	99
CREAMY TUSCAN CHICKEN	101
LEMON SOY ROASTED BRANZINO	103

INTRODUCTION

It's not a dream—there is a diet where you can eat all the cheese, eggs, and bacon you want. It's called the ketogenic diet, and it's a high-fat, moderate-protein, low-carb eating plan that could help you lose weight. This book includes just the recipes you need for your dinner meal; try one of these keto dinner recipe ideas. These mind-blowing keto dinner recipes not only get the low carb, high fat thing right, but they also come together in minutes, giving you plenty of time to go out and live your best keto life.

KETO CHICKEN DIANE

Prep Time: 10 Minutes

Cook Time: 15 Minutes

Serves: 4

Chicken Diane is a variation of the famous steak Diane recipe. It's made with succulent chicken breasts sautéed in butter and a creamy mushroom sauce. While this dish has a posh reputation, it's simple enough to prepare even on a busy weekday. In addition, this dish is inherently gluten-free and low in carbohydrates, making it versatile enough to fit into a variety of diets.

Ingredients

- 8 ounces mushrooms
- 2 cloves garlic
- 2 tablespoons unsalted butter
- pepper to taste

- 1-pound boneless, skinless chicken breasts
- Salt to taste
- 1/2 cup chicken stock
- 2 teaspoons Dijon mustard
- 2 tablespoons brandy
- 2 tablespoons heavy whipping cream
- 1 tablespoon freshly squeezed lemon juice
- 1 tablespoon fresh parsley minced

Instructions

1. In a large skillet, melt 1 tablespoon of butter over medium-high heat. Season the chicken on both sides with salt and pepper before placing it in the skillet.
2. Cook for three-four minutes until golden brown, then flip and cook for another two-three minutes. The chicken should be golden brown on all sides, no longer pink in the center, and the internal temperature should reach 165°F when measured with a meat thermometer. To keep warm, transfer to a plate and cover with foil.
3. Add the remaining tablespoon of butter to the skillet and return it to the fire. Cook, stirring regularly, for two to three minutes after adding the mushrooms.
4. Combine the garlic, lemon juice, parsley, and Dijon mustard in a mixing bowl. Cook for thirty seconds. If using, carefully pour in the brandy.
5. Cook for another minute or two to heat through the stock.
6. Whisk in the cream slowly. Season with salt and pepper to taste, if necessary.
7. Return the chicken to the pan, along with any accumulated juices. Place the sauce and mushrooms on top of the chicken.
8. Serve with veggies on the side or over pasta, rice, zoodles, cauliflower rice, or any other base of your choice.

Nutrition

Calories: 251 | Carbohydrates: 4g | Fiber: 1g | Sugar: 2g | Protein: 27g

Fat: 12g | Saturated Fat: 6g | Cholesterol: 99mg

CREAMY LEMON ARTICHOKE CHICKEN

Prep Time: 10 Minutes

Cook Time: 20 Minutes

Serves: 6

Fresh, creamy, and bursting with flavor, this Creamy Lemon Artichoke Chicken is a must-try. It's an easy one-pan meal with seared chicken, marinated artichoke hearts, cream, and lemon. This easy recipe is inherently low carb, keto-friendly, and gluten-free.

Ingredients

- 2 tablespoons unsalted butter
- 2 cloves garlic
- 1.5 pounds boneless, skinless chicken breasts
- 1 small shallot minced
- salt to taste

- pepper to taste
- 2 teaspoons freshly squeezed lemon juice
- 14 ounces marinated artichoke hearts
- 1 cup white wine
- 1/4 cup heavy cream
- thyme, dill, basil, or parsley optional
- lemon slices optional

Instructions

1. Season the chicken on both sides with salt and pepper.
2. In a large skillet over medium-high heat, melt 1 tablespoon of butter.
3. In a skillet, brown the chicken. Cook for three-four minutes on each side, or until golden brown and no longer pink in the middle. To keep warm, transfer to a dish and cover with foil.
4. Return the pan to the stovetop over medium heat after wiping it clean.
5. Add the garlic, shallot, and artichokes to the remaining butter and stir to combine. To soften, cook for two-three minutes.
6. Pour in the white wine with care, bring to a boil, and reduce by half.
7. Combine the heavy cream and 1 teaspoon lemon juice in a mixing bowl. Taste and adjust the seasoning with more lemon juice or heavy cream if necessary.
8. Return the chicken to the pan, along with any accumulated juices, and heat thoroughly.
9. If preferred, garnish with fresh thyme, dill, basil, or parsley, as well as lemon slices.

Nutrition

Calories: 307 | Carbohydrates: 6g | Protein: 25g | Fiber: 1g | Sugar: 1g

Fat: 16g | Saturated Fat: 6g | Cholesterol: 96mg

SPAGHETTI SQUASH CACIO E PEPE

Prep Time: 10 Minutes

Cook Time: 40 Minutes

Serves: 4

Cacio e Pepe with Spaghetti Squash is a lighter variation of the classic Italian Cacio e Pepe. Instead of pasta, spaghetti squash is used to make this similarly cheesy and peppery dish that is low in calories, carbs, and gluten-free.

Ingredients

- 2 tablespoons unsalted butter
- 1 cup pecorino Romano cheese
- 1 tablespoon extra-virgin olive oil

- 1 medium spaghetti squash about 4 cups
- salt and pepper to taste

Instructions

1. Preheat the oven to 425 degrees Fahrenheit.
2. Cut the squash in half carefully and scrape off the seeds and pulp. Place the cookies on a baking pan.
3. Season with salt and pepper after brushing with olive oil.
4. Roast for thirty-forty minutes, or until squash is soft and beginning to caramelize.
5. Allow the squash to cool to room temperature before scraping the strands from the skin with a fork. In a serving bowl, combine all of the ingredients.
6. Melt the butter in the microwave or over low heat in a small sauce pan.
7. Stir the squash with the melted butter and toss thoroughly. Stir in half to three-quarters of the cheese, saving the remainder for topping.
8. Serve the spaghetti squash with additional cheese and fresh cranberries on top.

Nutrition

Calories: 200 | Carbohydrates: 6g | Protein: 8g | Fiber: 1g | Sugar: 2g

Fat: 16g | Cholesterol: 41mg

KETO CREAMY CHICKEN PICCATA

Prep Time: 10 Minutes

Cook Time: 20 Minutes

Serves: 4

Keto Creamy Chicken Piccata is a gluten-free, low-carb version of conventional chicken piccata with a cream-based sauce. Pan-fried chicken slices dredged in almond flour are served with a spicy, creamy butter sauce. This dish is equally as delectable as the original, quick to prepare and suitable for the whole family.

Ingredients

Chickcn

- 1.5 pounds boneless, skinless chicken breasts
- 1/2 cup blanched almond flour
- 2 tablespoons extra virgin olive oil
- 2 tablespoons unsalted butter

- 1/2 teaspoon salt
- 1/4 teaspoon pepper

Creamy Piccata Sauce

- 4 cloves garlic minced
- 1 tablespoon unsalted butter
- 1 shallot
- 1 cup white wine
- 1/4 cup capers
- 2 tablespoons heavy cream
- 1/4 cup fresh squeezed lemon juice
- fresh parsley (optional)

Instructions

1. On a plate or in a small bowl, combine the almond flour, salt, and pepper. Place the chicken on a second dish after dredging it in the flour mixture.
2. In a large skillet over medium-high heat, melt 1 tablespoon of butter and 1 tablespoon of olive oil. Add half of the chicken once the butter-oil mixture is heated and sizzles when water is sprayed over it.
3. Cook for about two to three minutes, until golden brown, then turn and cook for another two minutes, or until the bottom is golden brown and the chicken is cooked through. Transfer to a plate that has been cleaned. Continue with the remaining butter, olive oil, and chicken.
4. Cook for about two to three minutes, until golden brown, then turn and cook for another two minutes, or until the bottom is golden brown and the chicken is cooked through. Remove to a clean plate. Continue with the remaining butter, olive oil, and chicken.
5. Reduce the heat to medium-low and stir in 1 tablespoon of butter. Once the butter has melted, add the shallots and garlic and simmer for two minutes, or until softened.
6. Pour in the wine gradually, increase the heat, and bring to a boil. Sweep up any browned bits as you reduce them by half.
7. Add the lemon juice, capers, and heavy cream once the sauce has reduced. Stir everything together thoroughly. Return the chicken to the pan, along with any accumulated juices, to warm through. If desired, serve the chicken with spoonful of piccata sauce on top and fresh parsley on the side.

Nutrition

Calories: 500 | Carbohydrates: 8g | Fiber: 2g | Sugar: 2g | Protein: 40g

Fat: 30g | Cholesterol: 142mg

LOADED BELL PEPPER NACHOS

Prep Time: 15 Minutes

Cook Time: 10 Minutes

Serves: 6

Low-carb, keto-friendly Loaded Bell Pepper Nachos are a low-carb, keto-friendly alternative to traditional Mexican nachos. This healthy recipe just takes 30 minutes to prepare and be eaten as a snack or a supper.

Ingredients

Bell Pepper Nachos

- 1 tablespoon chili powder
- 1-pound ground beef
- 2 teaspoons ground cumin
- 2 pounds bell peppers

- 1 1/2 cups sharp cheddar cheese
- 1 teaspoon salt
- 1/2 teaspoon pepper
- 1/2 teaspoon dried oregano

Nacho Toppings

- 1 jalapeño pepper
- 1/4 cup cilantro finely chopped
- 10 cherry tomatoes
- 1/2 cup guacamole
- 1/2 cup sour cream

Instructions

1. Preheat the oven to 400 degrees Fahrenheit.
2. Combine the ground beef, chili powder, cumin, oregano, salt, and pepper in a large skillet over medium-high heat. Cook, breaking up occasionally, until the meat is no longer pink, about five-seven minutes.
3. Place the bell pepper pieces on a baking sheet, cut side up, and spread them out as much as possible.
4. Fill each pepper with the ground beef mixture. Then, add the cheddar cheese on top.
5. Bake for five-seven minutes, or until completely melted cheese. The peppers must be heated but not mushy.
6. Remove the nachos from the oven and serve with cherry tomato slices, jalapeno pepper slices, cilantro, sour cream, and guacamole on top.

Nutrition

Calories: 377 | Carbohydrates: 14g | Fiber: 5g | Sugar: 8g | Protein: 25g

Fat: 25g | Saturated Fat: 12g | Cholesterol: 89mg

KETO BEEF STROGANOFF

Prep Time: 10 Minutes

Cook Time: 25 Minutes

Serves: 8

Beef Stroganoff is created with extremely soft beef pieces and mushroom slices in a rich, creamy, and delicious sauce. This dish may be kept low carb and gluten-free by making a few modest changes to the conventional form.

Ingredients

- 1/2 cup shallot finely diced
- 1-pound mushrooms
- 3 tablespoons unsalted butter
- 1 cup demi-glace
- 2 pounds beef tenderloin tips

- 1 tablespoon Dijon mustard
- 1 cup heavy cream
- 1 cup sour cream
- 1 tablespoon fresh parsley minced
- salt to taste
- pepper to taste

Instructions

1. In a large skillet, melt the butter. Brown all sides of the beef tenderloin tips until medium-rare or as desired. To keep warm, transfer to a dish and cover with foil.
2. Cook, stirring regularly until the shallots are softened, about two-three minutes.
3. Add the mushrooms and simmer for three-four minutes, or until the pan is nearly dry.
4. Bring the demi-glace to a boil, then reduce to low heat and cook for about ten minutes.
5. Combine the heavy whipping cream, sour cream, Dijon mustard, tenderloin, and any remaining juices in a large mixing bowl. Warm for a minute or two in the oven.
6. Season to taste with salt and pepper, if desired.
7. Serve over egg noodles, fried potatoes, or cauliflower rice, zoodles, or spaghetti squash.

Nutrition

Calories: 611 | Carbohydrates: 14g | Fiber: 1g | Sugar: 6g | Protein: 32g

Fat: 47g | Saturated Fat: 23g | Cholesterol: 146mg

RANCH CHICKEN MEATBALLS

Prep Time: 10 Minutes

Cook Time: 20 Minutes

Serves: 4

Ranch Chicken Meatballs are flavorful and easy to make with only four ingredients. These may be served as an appetizer or a main course, and they're great for entertaining, particularly at football and Super Bowl parties.

Ingredients

- 2 tablespoons dry Ranch seasoning
- 1-pound ground chicken
- 3/4 cup blanched almond flour
- 1 egg

Instructions

1. Preheat the oven to 400 degrees Fahrenheit. If preferred, line a baking sheet with aluminum foil or parchment paper.
2. In a large mixing bowl, combine the ground chicken, almond flour, Ranch seasoning, and egg until combined. If the mixture is too wet, gradually add more almond flour.
3. Form 24 1-inch meatballs with your hands, a tiny ice cream scoop, or a melon baller, and place them on the baking sheet.
4. Bake for twenty-twenty five minutes, or until thoroughly cooked.
5. If desired, serve with a side of Ranch dressing for dipping.

Nutrition

Calories: 317 | Carbohydrates: 9g | Fiber: 2g | Sugar: 1g | Protein: 26g

Fat: 21g | Saturated Fat: 4g | Cholesterol: 138mg

KETO PORK PICCATA

Prep Time: 10 Minutes

Cook Time: 20 Minutes

Serves: 4

Pork Piccata is a gluten-free, low-carb version of popular chicken piccata. Pork chops are pan-fried after being dredged in almond flour. They're then covered with a butter sauce made with lemon zest and capers.

Ingredients

Fried Pork Chops

- 1.5 pounds pork chops
- 1 tablespoon butter
- 1/2 cup blanched almond flour
- 1/2 teaspoon salt

- 1/4 teaspoon pepper
- 1 tablespoon extra-virgin olive oil

Piccata Sauce

- 4 cloves garlic minced
- 1 cup white wine
- 1/4 cup capers
- 1 tablespoon unsalted butter
- 1 shallot diced
- 1/4 cup lemon juice
- fresh parsley (optional)

Instructions

Fried Pork Chops

1. On a plate or in a small bowl, combine the almond flour, salt, and pepper.
2. Place the pork on a plate after dredging it in the almond flour mixture.
3. In a large skillet, melt 1 tablespoon of butter and 1 tablespoon of olive oil over medium-high heat. Add the pork once the butter-oil mixture is heated and sizzles when water is sprayed over it.
4. Cook for three to four minutes until golden brown on the bottom, then flip and cook for another two to three minutes or until the pork is cooked through.
5. Place on a clean dish.

Piccata Sauce

1. Reduce the heat to medium-low and stir in the remaining 1 tablespoon butter. Once the butter has melted, add the shallots and garlic and simmer for two minutes, or until softened.
2. Pour in the wine gradually, increase the heat, and bring to a boil. Scrape up any browned bits as you reduce by half.
3. Stir in the lemon juice and capers once the sauce has been reduced.
4. Return the pork to the pan to finish cooking.
5. If desired, serve the pork chops with spoonful of piccata sauce on top and fresh parsley on the side.

Nutrition

Calories: 488 | Carbohydrates: 8g | Fiber: 2g | Sugar: 2g | Protein: 40g

Fat: 28g | Cholesterol: 129mg | Sodium: 680mg

CHIPOTLE CHEDDAR CAULIFLOWER "MAC AND CHEESE"

Prep Time: 10 Minutes

Cook Time: 15 Minutes

Serves: 4

Cheddar Chipotle Roasted cauliflower is mixed in a smoky, creamy cheddar cheese sauce to make cauliflower. It can be served as a main dish or a side dish that is keto-friendly and gluten-free.

Ingredients

Roasted Cauliflower

- 1 large head cauliflower cut into florets
- 1/2 teaspoon salt
- 1 tablespoon extra-virgin olive oil

- 1 tablespoon butter
- 1/4 cup blanched almond flour
- Toasted Almond Flour Crumbs
- 1/4 teaspoon pepper

Chipotle Cheddar Sauce

- 3/4 cup heavy cream
- 1-ounce cream cheese
- 1 tablespoon butter
- 1 teaspoon chipotle chili powder
- green onions or parsley optional
- 1 cup cheddar cheese shredded

Instructions

Roasted Cauliflower

1. Preheat the oven to 425 degrees Fahrenheit. Spread the cauliflower florets out on a sheet pan and toss them with olive oil. Then salt & pepper to taste.
2. Roast for fifteen minutes, or until fork-tender, tossing halfway through.

Toasted Almond Flour Crumbs

Make the almond flour crumbs while the cauliflower is roasting. In a small saucepan, melt 1 tablespoon of butter, then add the almond flour. Cook, tossing regularly, for about two to three minutes, or until lightly browned. Remove the pan from the heat and set it aside to cool.

Chipotle Cheddar Sauce

1. In a medium saucepan, melt the remaining butter. Stir in cream cheese and heavy cream until melted and hot. Remove the pan from the heat and stir in the chipotle chili powder and cheddar cheese until smooth.
2. When the cauliflower is done roasting, put it with the cheese sauce in a skillet and stir to combine.
3. If desired, serve topped with the almond flour crumbs and a garnish of sliced green onions or parsley.

Nutrition

Calories: 439 | Carbohydrates: 9g | Protein: 12g | Fiber: 3g | Sugar: 3g

Fat: 41g | Cholesterol: 114mg

KETO MEXICAN BEEF BOWLS

Prep Time: 10 Minutes

Cook Time: 20 Minutes

Serves: 4

Riced cauliflower, wonderfully seasoned ground beef, and a quick homemade salsa make up these Keto Mexican Beef Bowls. To add even more flavor, top them with crumbled queso or cotija cheese and tangy lime mayo. These bowls are low carb, keto-friendly, and gluten-free and take only 30 minutes to prepare.

Ingredients

<u>Quick Salsa</u>

- 2 tablespoons pickled jalapeno peppers
- 1 cup tomato
- 1 tablespoon lime juice

Mexican Beef Bowls

- 1-pound ground beef
- 1 tablespoon extra-virgin olive oil
- 1 tablespoon chili powder
- 1 medium head cauliflower about 4 cups
- 1/2 teaspoon dried oregano
- 1 teaspoon ground cumin
- 1/4 cup queso fresco
- 1 teaspoon salt
- 1/4 teaspoon pepper

Lime Mayonnaise

- 1 teaspoon lime juice
- 1 tablespoon mayonnaise

Instructions

Quick Salsa

In a small bowl, combine the tomato, jalapenos, and lime juice; set aside.

Mexican Beef Bowls

1. In a large skillet, heat the olive oil over medium-high heat. Cook, frequently tossing, until the cauliflower is soft, about three-seven minutes.
2. Meanwhile, season the ground beef with chili powder, cumin, oregano, salt, and pepper in a large skillet over medium heat.
3. Cook for about ten minutes, stirring frequently and breaking up larger chunks as needed until the beef is cooked through and no longer pink in the middle.
4. Divide the cauliflower evenly between four bowls to assemble the bowls. Top with equal amounts of the Mexican beef, salsa, and crumbled cheese

Lime Mayonnaise

To prepare the Lime Mayonnaise, combine the mayonnaise and lime juice in a small mixing dish and pour over each bowl immediately before serving.

Nutrition

Calories: 331 | Carbohydrates: 11g | Protein: 28g | Fiber: 4g | Sugar: 4g

Fat: 20g | Saturated Fat: 7g | Cholesterol: 80mg

KETO MAPLE WALNUT SALMON

Prep Time: 5 Minutes

Cook Time: 15 Minutes

Serves: 4

Maple Walnut Salmon is a simple dish that only requires a few ingredients and is naturally gluten-free and low carb. This delectable dish boasts a crispy texture, sweet and spicy flavors, and a slew of health benefits.

Ingredients

- 4-ounce fillets salmon
- 1 tablespoon pure maple syrup
- salt and pepper to taste
- 1/2 cup chopped walnuts
- 1 tablespoon Dijon mustard

- 1/4 teaspoon onion powder
- 1/4 teaspoon smoked paprika
- fresh parsley optional

Instructions

1. Preheat the oven to 400 degrees Fahrenheit.
2. Place the salmon skin-side down on a baking sheet lined with parchment paper or aluminum foil. Using paper towels, pat dry and season with salt and pepper.
3. Combine the walnuts, maple syrup, Dijon mustard, smoked paprika, and onion powder in a small mixing bowl and stir well. Gently pat down the walnut mixture onto the tops of the salmon fillets.
4. Depending on the thickness of your fillets, bake for twelve-fifteen minutes or until the salmon is opaque and easily flaked off with a fork.
5. If desired, garnish with fresh parsley.

Nutrition

Calories: 273 | Carbohydrates: 6g | Fiber: 1g | Sugar: 3g | Protein: 25g

Fat: 17g | Saturated Fat: 2g | Cholesterol: 62mg

PIZZA BIANCA (WHITE PIZZA) WITH SUN-DRIED TOMATOES AND BROCCOLI

Prep Time: 20 Minutes

Cook Time: 15 Minutes

Serves: 6

Pizza Bianca, also known as White Pizza, is a sauce-free pizza with various Italian cheeses on top. Sun-dried tomatoes and broccoli have been added to this recipe, served on a low-carb cauliflower crust for additional taste. However, any pizza dough can be used.

Ingredients

- 1 1/2 cups ricotta cheese
- 1/2 cup mozzarella cheese
- 1 Cauliflower Pizza Crust
- 6 cloves roasted garlic

- 1/2 cup sun-dried tomatoes
- 1 cup broccoli florets
- salt and pepper to taste

Instructions

1. Preheat your oven according to the instructions on your pizza crust recipe.
2. Up to the first bake, prepare your pizza crust.
3. To make a paste, mash the roasted garlic cloves. Combine the ricotta cheese, mozzarella cheese, and garlic in a medium mixing bowl and mix thoroughly. Season lightly with salt and pepper.
4. Apply the cheese mixture to the pizza crust in the same way as you would pizza sauce.
5. Sun-dried tomatoes and broccoli go on top.
6. Return the pizza to the oven for another five-seven minutes, or until the crust is crisp and heated toppings.
7. Serve warm, cut into 6 slices.

Nutrition

Calories: 266 | Carbohydrates: 15g | Protein: 19g | Fiber: 4g | Sugar: 6g

Fat: 15g | Cholesterol: 79mg

KETO MAC AND CHEESE WITH ZOODLES

Prep Time: 10 Minutes

Cook Time: 20 Minutes

Serves: 4

This Keto Mac and Cheese recipe have only 5 grams of carbs per serving so that you can enjoy this comfort food favorite guilt-free! Spiralized zucchini is tossed in a thick, creamy cheese sauce.

Ingredients

- 8 ounces sharp cheddar cheese
- 2 ounces cream cheese
- 1 teaspoon mustard powder
- 4 cups zucchini
- 1/2 teaspoon salt

- 1/2 cup heavy cream
- 1/4 teaspoon pepper
- 4 tablespoons butter

Instructions

1. In a large skillet, melt the butter over medium heat.
2. Cook, constantly stirring, until the cream cheese and heavy whipping cream are well combined about five minutes.
3. Salt, pepper, and mustard powder are added, followed by the cheddar cheese.
4. Cook for another two-three minutes, or until the cheese is completely melted and well combined.
5. Continue to simmer for another three-five minutes, or until the zucchini is barely soft. Serve immediately.

Nutrition

Calories: 503 | Carbohydrates: 6g | Fiber: 1g | Sugar: 3g | Protein: 17g

Fat: 46g | Cholesterol: 145mg

SMOKED SALMON EGG POTS

Prep Time: 15 Minutes

Cook Time: 20 Minutes

Serves: 4

This smoked salmon egg pot dish is high in protein. Serve with buttery toast soldiers for a warm weekend spread.

Ingredients

- 250g smoked salmon slices
- 6 large British Lion eggs, beaten
- 1 tablespoon chives, chopped
- A little oil
- A little lemon juices
- Salt and black pepper

- 3 tablespoons crème fraiche
- 1 tablespoon horseradish sauce
- Salad leaves to serve
- Salt and black pepper

Instructions

1. Preheat the oven to 180°C / 160°C fan / Gas Mark 4 / Use a little oil to grease four ramekins, then line the insides of each ramekin with smoked salmon, leaving some hanging over the edges to cover the tops later.
2. Cut any remaining salmon into small pieces and combine the beaten eggs and chives once the pan is lined. Season with salt and black pepper to taste.
3. Pour the egg mixture into the ramekins, then fold in the salmon lightly.
4. Place the ramekins on a baking pan, fill it with water to a depth of about 5cm, and bake for fifteen-twenty minutes, or until set and firm to the touch.
5. Combine the crème fraiche, horseradish, lemon juice, and black pepper in a mixing bowl to make the cheat's hollandaise.
6. Remove the eggs from the water and place them upside down on a plate. Remove the ramekin from the pot. Serve with salad leaves and hollandaise sauce.

Nutrition

Calories: 285 | Carbohydrates: 1.4g | Salt: 1.1g | Protein: 27.8g | Fat 18.9g

Saturated 7.9g

GLUTEN-FREE, LOW CARB & KETO FISH AND CHIPS

Prep Time: 20 Minutes

Cook Time: 15 Minutes

Marinate: 120 Minutes

Serves: 2

We're talking gluten-free and keto fish and chips that are crisp, flaky, and soothing to boot! This low-carb version of the British classic is simple to make and will leave you wanting more.

Ingredients

For the gluten-free & keto fish tacos

- 250 g firm white-flesh fish, preferably cod
- 4 cloves of garlic ran through a press
- 1/2 cup whey protein isolate

- 1 teaspoon baking powder
- 2 teaspoons apple cider vinegar
- 1/4 teaspoon garlic powder
- 1/3 cup sour cream
- 1/4-1/2 teaspoon kosher salt to taste
- kosher salt to taste
- 1 tablespoon sour cream or coconut cream
- 2 teaspoons apple cider vinegar
- 1 egg
- coconut oil or cooking oil of choice

For Serving

- 1 batch of our keto mayonnaise
- 1 batch jicama fries 8 tortillas
- vinegar
- lemon

Instructions

1. Combine sour cream, vinegar, and garlic in a mixing bowl. Season with salt to taste. Cut the fish into 2-inch broad strips across the grain of the flesh and place them in the cream marinade. Refrigerate for at least two hours, ideally overnight.
2. Make a batch of jicama fries that are low in carbs and high in flavor.
3. Add enough oil to a skillet or pan to make it about 1/2-inch deep for your frying station. By utilizing a narrower pan and cooking in batches, you may save a lot of oil. While coating the fish, heat the oil over medium/low heat.
4. Combine the whey protein, baking powder, garlic powder, and salt in a shallow plate or dish. Whisk the egg, cream, and vinegar together in a second plate or dish.
5. Coat the fish by removing excess marinade, immersing it in the egg mixture, the whey protein mixture, and immediately placing it in the heated oil and basting it. For the finest crispness, cook the fish right after coating. Fry until deeply golden on both sides, then transfer to a paper-lined plate to cool for a few minutes.
6. Serve right away over a bed of jicama fries, plenty of lemons, mayonnaise, and a drizzle of vinegar.

Nutrition

Calories: 242 | Carbohydrates: 1g | Sugar: 1g | Protein: 26g | Fat: 13g

Saturated Fat: 6g | Cholesterol: 158mg

LOW CARB CHICKEN AND CAULIFLOWER LASAGNE

Prep Time: 40 Minutes

Cook Time: 60 Minutes

Serves: 8

A nutritious supper may be made by combining this delicious cauliflower and three-cheese chicken lasagne recipe.

Ingredients

- 500-gram chicken mince
- 200-gram mushroom button, sliced
- 1 leek trimmed, thinly sliced
- 1 bunch spinach trimmed, chopped
- 1 tablespoon olive oil
- 125 ml tomato pasta sauce
- 250-gram cream cheese chopped
- 100-gram mozzarella grated

- 1 teaspoon dried tarragon

Cauliflower Lasagne Sheets

- 1.1 kg cauliflower trimmed
- 2 eggs
- 40-gram grated parmesan

Instructions

1. Process half of the cauliflower in a food processor until finely chopped for the cauliflower lasagne sheets.
2. Into a microwave-safe bowl, transfer the mixture. Carry on with the rest of the cauliflower.
3. Cover and microwave on high for ten minutes, or until soft, stirring frequently.
4. Drain through a fine strainer, return to the bowl, and toss in the egg and parmesan cheese until thoroughly combined.
5. Season with salt and pepper and mix well to combine.
6. Preheat the oven to 180 degrees Celsius.
7. Using the baking paper, line two large baking trays.
8. Divide the cauliflower mixture between the prepared trays and gently press each batch into a rectangle measuring 22 x 30 cm with your fingertips (8 x 12 inches).
9. Cook for twenty minutes or until the liquid has evaporated.
10. Allow cooling before serving. Cut the lasagna sheets into 4-inch-wide sheets.
11. Heat the oil in a large nonstick frying pan over high heat, then add the leek and cook, constantly turning, for 4 minutes, or until tender.
12. Increase the heat to high and cook the chicken for five minutes, breaking it up with a wooden spoon as it cooks. Add the mushrooms and cook, frequently stirring, for five minutes, or until browned. Add the spinach and cook, stirring regularly, for four minutes, or until wilted.
13. Whisk in the cream cheese for two minutes, until it has melted, then stir in the tarragon and season to taste. Set aside. Preheat the oven to 350°F and grease a 7 x 9-inch square baking dish. Top with half of the chicken mixture and sprinkle with ⅓ cup mozzarella. Repeat with the leftover chicken mixture and another layer of cauliflower. Finish with the remaining lasagna. Finish with a dollop of spaghetti sauce and some mozzarella. Bake for thirty minutes or until golden brown, then set aside to cool for seven minutes before serving.

Nutrition

Calories: 344 | Carbohydrates: 13g | Protein: 24g | Fiber: 4g | Sugar: 5g | Fat: 23g
Saturated Fat: 11g | Cholesterol: 143mg

LOW-CARB PALMINI CARBONARA WITH KALE AND SAUSAGES

Prep Time: 2 Minutes

Cook Time: 8 Minutes

Serves: 4

Palmini Carbonara is a Keto dieter's, and pasta lover's fantasy come true. Hearts of palm noodles, kale, and sausages are thrown in a cheesy egg mixture for a delicious dish.

Ingredients

- 1 packet Palmini Pasta

Kale & Sausages

- 1 teaspoon Garlic, Minced
- 1 cup Kale, Shredded
- 2 links Chicken Sausages, Precooked

- 1 teaspoon Butter

Sauce

- ¼ teaspoon Black Pepper
- ¼ teaspoon Garlic Powder
- 2 Eggs
- 2 teaspoon Parsley, Chopped
- ¼ cup Shredded Mozzarella
- ¼ teaspoon Italian seasoning

Instructions

1. Palmini will be drained and rinsed well with cold water.
2. Bring 1 inch of water to a simmer in the skillet. Cook, constantly tossing, until the kale is bright green, tender, and wilted for about 2 minutes. Remove any excess water.
3. Toss in the garlic and butter for thirty seconds. Set aside.
4. Slice the sausage into 18" thick coins.
5. Add 2-3 tablespoons of water and the sausages in a skillet and cook for about a minute on each side. Set aside.
6. Whisk together the egg, seasonings, and cheese in a small bowl.
7. Palmini must be heated in the microwave for around one and half minutes on high.
8. Reduce heat to low and mix in 1-2 tablespoons water, palming, greens, and sausages.
9. Toss in the egg-cheese mixture with tongs rapidly to coat the pasta and prevent the egg from scrambling. If the pasta is still hot, the egg will cook.
10. If preferred, season with salt and serve with extra shredded mozzarella on top.

Nutrition

Calories: 272 | Fat: 15.5g | Fiber: 3.3g | Sugar: 0.2g | Protein: 24.9g

Saturated fat: 6.6g | Carbohydrates: 11.5g

LOW-CARB MOUSSAKA

Prep Time: 10 Minutes

Cook Time: 40 Minutes

Serves: 4

Our low-carb version of this Greek classic is juicier, cheesier, and packed with vegetables than the original, and it's also a lot faster and easier to make. After relishing this delicious dinner, even the Greek gods would lick their fingers.

Ingredients

- ¼ cup olive oil
- 1 lb. eggplant
- 1 teaspoon ground cinnamon
- 2 garlic cloves chopped
- 1 yellow onion chopped
- 1 teaspoon salt

- 1¼ lbs. ground chicken, or any other ground meat
- ½ cup tomato sauce
- 1 tablespoon paprika powder
- 1 tablespoon dried oregano
- ½ teaspoon ground black pepper

Cheese sauce

- ½ cup heavy whipping cream
- 1 garlic clove, pressed
- 2 cups shredded gouda cheese, divided
- 6 tablespoon cream cheese
- ¼ teaspoon salt
- ¼ teaspoon ground nutmeg optional

Serving

- 1½ cups leafy greens optional

Instructions

1. Preheat the oven to 350 degrees Fahrenheit
2. Peel the eggplant and cut it into small dices, about half an inch in size. Fry eggplant in olive oil in a large frying pan over medium heat. Season with salt and pepper.
3. Combine the onion, garlic, and spices in a mixing bowl. Cook for a few minutes, or until the onion and eggplant begin to soften and color.
4. Fry the ground meat until it is fully done. Simmer for a few minutes after adding the tomato sauce.
5. Combine the ingredients for the cheese sauce in a pot, reserving half of the cheese for the top! Allow thickening for a few minutes on low heat. If using, mix in the ground nutmeg well.
6. Place the meat in a big or several small baking dishes. Pour the sauce over the top and sprinkle the remaining cheese on top.
7. Place the cheese in the oven for about twenty minutes, or until it turns a lovely golden color. Serve with a salad of lush greens.

Nutrition

Calories: 762 | Carbohydrates: 11g | Protein: 43g | Fat: 60g

ONE-PAN PARMESAN CHICKEN DINNER

Prep Time: 15 Minutes

Cook Time: 25 Minutes

Serves: 4

All in one pan: saucy chicken, melted mozzarella, and crisp-tender broccoli. What could be better than that?

Ingredients

- 1/2 cup grated Parmesan cheese
- 1/2 cup panko bread crumbs
- 1 teaspoon garlic powder
- 1/2 teaspoon salt
- 1 teaspoon pepper
- 1 large egg

- 4 cups fresh or frozen broccoli florets
- 1 cup marinara sauce
- 1 cup shredded mozzarella cheese
- 4 boneless skinless chicken breast halves
- Olive oil-flavored cooking spray
- 1/4 cup minced fresh basil, optional

Instructions

1. Preheat the oven to 400 degrees Fahrenheit. Using cooking spray, lightly coat a 15x10x1-inch baking pan.
2. Whisk the egg in a small bowl. Stir together 1/2 cup panko bread crumbs, 1/2 cup grated Parmesan cheese, 1/2 teaspoon salt, 1 teaspoon pepper, and 1 teaspoon garlic powder in a separate shallow bowl. Allow excess egg to drop off the chicken breast. Then dip in the crumb mixture, rubbing it down to help the coating stick. Repeat with the rest of the chicken. Place the chicken breasts in the baking pan's center third. Using cooking spray, spritz the surface.
3. Bake for ten minutes in the oven. Remove the dish from the oven. Broccoli should be spread in a single layer along both edges of the sheet pan. Return to the oven and bake for another 10 minutes. Remove the dish from the oven.
4. Preheat broiler. Cover the chicken with marinara sauce and grated cheese. Broil the chicken and broccoli 3-4 inches from the fire for three-five minutes, or until the cheese is golden brown and the vegetables are soft. Sprinkle with basil, if desired.

Nutrition

Calories: 504 | Fat: 10g | Sugars: 7g | Fiber: 8g | Protein: 52g | Saturated Fat: 7g

Cholesterol: 147mg | Carbohydrate: 9g

HERBED BUTTER WHOLE ROASTED CHICKEN

Prep Time: 15 Minutes

Cook Time: 70 Minutes

Serves: 4

The juiciest chicken you'll ever bite into is this herbed butter entire roasted chicken. The butter and spice sandwiched between the skin and the breasts seals in the flavor and kept the chicken juicy throughout the cooking process.

Ingredients

- 2 teaspoons dried thyme
- 2 teaspoons rubbed sage
- 6 tablespoons butter, at room temperature
- 4-pound whole chicken

- 1 ½ cups chicken stock
- 2 teaspoons dried minced onion
- 1 teaspoon garlic powder
- ½ teaspoon black pepper
- 1 teaspoon sea salt

Instructions

1. Preheat the oven to 400 degrees Fahrenheit.
2. Combine the butter, thyme, sage, onion flakes, salt, garlic powder, and pepper in a small bowl. Mix until all of the ingredients are thoroughly combined.
3. In a shallow roasting pan, place the chicken breast side up. Pour the chicken stock into the roasting pan's bottom.
4. Gently loosen the skin covering the chicken breasts by moving it away from the breast and creating a pocket between the skin and the breast.
5. Sprinkle half of the herbed butter evenly between the skin and the breasts. Apply the remaining half of the herbed butter on the chicken's top.
6. Preheat oven to 350°F and bake for thirty minutes on the center rack. Remove the chicken from the oven, baste it with the juices, and return it to the oven. Roast for thirty to forty-five minutes more, basting every ten minutes.
7. Roast until the meat is cooked through and the skin is crisp, reaching 165°F on a meat thermometer.

Nutrition

Calories: 450 | Sugar: 0.3g | Fat: 33.9g | Fiber: 0.2g | Protein: 34g

Carbohydrates: 0.9g | Cholesterol: 179mg

BAKED CHICKEN WITH POTATOES & ONIONS

Prep Time: 15 Minutes

Cook Time: 50 Minutes

Serves: 6

This baked chicken with onions and garlic is a one-pan meal that can easily be made ahead of time and is excellent for a no-fuss weekday dinner.

It doesn't even require any side dishes because this one-pan contains everything you need for a well-balanced, nutritious supper.

Ingredients

- 1 cut-up chicken 3 to 3 1/2 pounds, should be 8 pieces and breasts halved crosswise
- 1 large onion cut into eighths
- 1-pound small potatoes halved

- 1 lemon quartered
- 2 sprigs fresh rosemary finely minced
- 1 head garlic clove separated and left unpeeled
- 3 tablespoons red wine vinegar
- 1/4 cup extra-virgin olive oil
- Kosher salt and ground pepper

Instructions

1. Preheat the oven to 450 degrees Fahrenheit. In a 12x16-inch glass roasting pan, arrange the chicken skin side up, potatoes, onions, garlic, and lemon.
2. Rosemary, salt, and pepper are used to season the chicken and vegetables.
3. Drizzle oil, vinegar, and a pinch of salt and pepper over the chicken and vegetables.
4. Cook for fifty minutes, or until the chicken is golden brown and well cooked. Enjoy!

Nutrition

Calories: 517 | Carbohydrates: 10g | Fiber: 3g | Sugar: 3g | Protein: 1g

Fat: 54g | Saturated Fat: 8g

CHICKEN VEGGIE PACKETS

Prep Time: 10 Minutes

Cook Time: 20 Minutes

Serves: 4

When these packages are served, people believe they went to great lengths to prepare them. Individual aluminum foil bags keep the herbed chicken moist and tender throughout baking by trapping the liquids. In addition, the foil saves time and facilitates cleanup.

Ingredients

- 4 boneless skinless chicken breast halves
- 1 cup pearl onions
- 1-1/2 cups fresh baby carrots
- 1/2 pound sliced fresh mushrooms
- 3 teaspoons minced fresh thyme

- 1/2 cup julienned sweet red pepper
- 1/4 teaspoon pepper
- Lemon wedges, optional
- 1/2 teaspoon salt, optional

Instructions

1. Preheat the oven to 375 degrees Fahrenheit. Flatten chicken breasts to 1/2-inch thickness and place on a heavy-duty foil sheet. Over the chicken, layer the mushrooms, carrots, onions, and red pepper; season with pepper, thyme, and salt, if preferred.
2. Seal the foil tightly around the chicken and vegetables. Place the cookies on a baking pan. Cook for about twenty minutes, or until the chicken juices flow clear. Serve with lemon wedges if preferred.

Nutrition

Calories: 175 | Fat: 3g | Saturated Fat: 1g | Sugar: 6g | Fiber: 2g | Protein: 25g

Cholesterol: 63mg | Carbohydrate: 9g

ROASTED SHRIMP AND GREEN BEANS

Prep Time: 10 Minutes

Cook Time: 10 Minutes

Serves: 4

This roasted shrimp and green beans recipe is a quick and healthful one-pan dish that mixes shrimp and fresh green beans with a simple, tasty marinade. The ideal quick supper option that is delicious, nutritious, and suitable for the whole family!

Ingredients

For the beans

- 1/2 teaspoon ground coriander
- 1 lb. green beans, trimmed and cut into bite-sized pieces
- 1 tablespoon extra-virgin olive oil

- 1/8 teaspoon cayenne pepper
- 1/4 teaspoon kosher salt
- 1/2 teaspoon ground cumin
- 1/2 teaspoon fresh ground black pepper

For the shrimp

- 1 tablespoon olive oil plus a little extra to brush on the roasting pan
- 1 lb. medium-large raw shrimp thawed if frozen, peeled
- zest from one lemon save the lemon and cut into fourths
- 1/2 teaspoon fresh ground black pepper
- 1/4 teaspoon kosher salt

Instructions

1. Preheat the oven to 425 degrees Fahrenheit.
2. Rinse the shrimp under cold water once it has been peeled and washed. Make sure the shrimp are completely dry before cooking.
3. Toss the green beans with extra virgin olive oil, ground coriander, ground cumin, salt, freshly ground black pepper, and cayenne pepper in a mixing bowl.
4. Combine the shrimp, extra virgin olive oil, lemon zest, salt, and freshly ground black pepper in a separate bowl.
5. Arrange green beans in a single layer on a roasting pan that has been brushed with olive oil or sprayed with nonstick spray. Green beans must be roasted for ten minutes. After ten minutes, combine the green beans with the shrimp and continue to roast for another eight-ten minute, or until the shrimp are just done.
6. Serve the shrimp and green beans right away with the four lemon quarters squeezed over them.

Nutrition

Calories: 212 | Carbohydrates: 8g | Protein: 25g | Fat: 9g | Fiber: 3g | Sugar: 4g

Saturated Fat: 1g | Cholesterol: 286mg

BRUSSELS SPROUTS WITH APPLES AND BACON

Prep Time: 10 Minutes

Cook Time: 20 Minutes

Serves: 4

This recipe for Brussels Sprouts with Bacon and Apples is a simple, elegant side dish that's ideal for a festive meal or a quick evening meal.

Ingredients

- 1 small onion chopped
- 1 lb. Brussels sprouts trimmed and halved
- 1/4 cup chopped parsley dill
- 2 medium tart apples diced
- 1 tbsp organic butter

- 4 slices organic bacon
- Salt and pepper to taste

Instructions

1. Cover the bacon with a paper towel and place it on a microwave-safe plate. Cook the bacon for four minutes, or until it's nice and crispy.
2. In a large sauté pan, melt butter and sauté onion with a bit of salt.
3. Place Brussels sprouts in a steamer basket and steam for eight to ten minutes, or until they are lovely and tender, while the onion is cooking.
4. Toss in the apples and simmer for another four to five minutes after your onions have become transparent. You want your apples to become a wonderful brown color and become just slightly soft.
5. Toss in the Brussels sprouts and season with salt and pepper once the apples and onions are finished. Toss the Brussels sprouts with the bacon crumbles and parsley. Season to taste, then savor.

Nutrition

Calories: 225 | Carbohydrates: 11g | Fiber: 7g | Sugar: 13g | Protein: 7g

Fat: 12g | Saturated Fat: 5g | Cholesterol: 22mg

KETO BOK CHOY - GINGER STIR-FRY

Prep Time: 5 Minutes

Cook Time: 10 Minutes

Serves: 2

This quick and easy Bok Choy Stir Fry is a fantastic side dish for chicken, fish, or tofu and takes only 15 minutes to prepare.

Ingredients

- 1 tablespoon low sodium soy sauce
- 1 teaspoon grated ginger
- 2 cloves garlic chopped
- 1 tablespoon coconut oil
- 1-pound bok choy

- toasted sesame seeds
- salt and pepper to taste

Instructions

1. Cool water, wash the bok choy and cut it up, separating the stems from the leaves.
2. In a large nonstick sauce pan, heat the olive oil and add garlic and ginger. Cook for about a minute or until aromatic. Cook for 5 minutes with bok choy stems, soy sauce, and a splash of water.
3. Toss in the bok choy leaves once the stems are cooked and simmer until they have wilted down.
4. Finish with a sprinkle of toasted sesame seeds and a dash of salt and pepper. Enjoy

Nutrition

Calories: 99 | Carbohydrates: 7g | Fiber: 2g | Sugar: 3g | Protein: 4g

Fat: 7g | Saturated Fat: 6g

CHICKEN ENCHILADA SKILLET

Prep Time: 5 Minutes

Cook Time: 25 Minutes

Serves: 6

The greatest part of chicken enchiladas is a low-carb dinner recipe that takes around 30 minutes to prepare.

Ingredients

- 2 tablespoons salted butter
- 1 1/2 pounds boneless, skinless chicken breasts cut into large chunks
- 1 tablespoon chili powder
- 1 cup chicken broth
- 2 tablespoons tomato paste
- 3/4 cup sour cream
- 1/8 teaspoon cayenne pepper

- 1/2 teaspoon garlic powder
- 1/2 teaspoon ground cumin
- 1 1/2 cups shredded cheddar cheese or Mexican cheese blend
- Cauliflower rice and your favorite enchilada toppings
- Salt and pepper

Instructions

1. Melt the butter in a large skillet over medium heat. Season the chicken with salt and pepper to taste. Brown the chicken in the butter for about 2 minutes per side.
2. Bring the broth to a low simmer. Cook for twelve to fifteen minutes, or until chicken is thoroughly done.
3. Remove half of the stock from the skillet and place the chicken on a plate. The broth will be discarded. In the same skillet, whisk the tomato paste, chili powder, garlic powder, cumin, and cayenne. With two forks, shred the chicken.
4. Reduce to low heat and whisk in the sour cream until smooth. Add the chicken and mix well. Cover the skillet with a lid and cook until the cheese has melted for about 4 minutes.
5. Serve with cauliflower rice and enchilada toppings such as pickled jalapenos, cilantro, guacamole, and tomatoes.

Nutrition

Calories: 343 | Fat: 22g | Saturated Fat: 12g | Sugar: 1g | Protein: 32g

Cholesterol: 127mg | Carbohydrates: 3g

KETO CRAB ALFREDO

Prep Time: 10 Minutes

Cook Time: 20 Minutes

Serves: 4

Thanks to the use of authentic Konjac noodles, this Keto Crab Alfredo Recipe is a big success with seafood enthusiasts and a perfect keto-friendly alternative to pasta meals.

Ingredients

- 6 tablespoons Grass-Fed Butter
- 16 Ounces of Konjac Fettuccini Noodles
- 1/4 Cup Grated Parmesan Cheese
- 8 Ounces Lump Snow Crab Meat
- 2 Cups Heavy Whipping Cream
- 1-2 teaspoons Xanthan Gum
- 1/4 Cup Grated Romano Cheese

- 1/2 teaspoon Crushed Red Pepper Flakes
- 1/2 teaspoon Pink Himalayan Salt
- 1/4 teaspoon Black Pepper
- 1 & 1/2 teaspoons Minced Garlic

Instructions

1. Prepare the dish by chopping fresh parsley and grating the Romano and Parmesan cheeses. Set them aside for the time being.
2. In a Large Sauce, Pan over Medium Heat melt 6 Tablespoons of Grass-Fed Butter
3. Once the butter has melted, add 1 to 2 teaspoons of Xanthan Gum to the mixture. The thicker the sauce becomes, the more you use it. The sauce will be thinner if you use less.
4. Pour in 2 Cups of Heavy Whipping Cream, and whisk together with the Butter and Xanthan Gum
5. Season the sauce with 2 Teaspoons of Dried Basil, 1 & 1/2 Teaspoons Minced Garlic, 1/2 Teaspoon Crushed Red Pepper Flakes, 1/2 Teaspoon Pink Himalayan Salt 1/4 Teaspoon, Black Pepper, while whisking the Heavy Cream.
6. Add 1/4 Cup grated Parmesan and 1/4 Cup Grated Romano pieces of cheese to the sauce, and stir them in well.
7. To bring the flavors together, cook the sauce for another minute. To thin or thicken the sauce to your desire, add more Heavy Whipping Cream or Xanthan Gum.
8. Add 8 ounces of Lump Snow Crab Meat and toss gently to mix without breaking up the crab meat chunks too much.
9. Remove the Sauce Pan from the heat and cover it.
10. Remove the Konjac Fettuccini Noodles from the liquid they were packaged in by opening the two packages and placing them in a strainer.
11. Place the noodles in a bowl of cold running water for one minute.
12. To warm the Konjac Noodles, place them on a microwave-safe plate and microwave for around two minutes.
13. Either serve the Konjac Noodles and top with the Crab Alfredo Sauce or combine everything together in the Sauce Pan.
14. Optionally, top with more of the chopped fresh parsley from earlier, as well as more grated cheeses if desired.

Nutrition

Calories: 670 | Fat: 60g | Sugar: 0.3g | Fiber: 5g | Protein: 17g | Cholesterol: 210mg

Sodium: 1020mg | Carbohydrates: 6g

BAKED - CREAMY BEEF NOODLE

Prep Time: 20 Minutes

Cook Time: 20 Minutes

Serves: 6

A layered casserole of tomato sauce seasoned ground beef, creamy egg noodles, and shredded cheese makes up Creamy Beef Noodle. It's made with simple ingredients and is a hit with the whole family.

Ingredients

- 1 lb. ground beef
- 2 cups cottage cheese
- 2 cups shredded cheese
- 1 package egg noodles
- 1/2 teaspoon onion powder

- 3/4 cup sour cream
- 1/2 teaspoon salt
- 1 can tomato sauce
- 1/4 teaspoon pepper

Instructions

- Preheat the oven to 350 degrees Fahrenheit. Spray a 9x13 baking dish with nonstick cooking spray.
- In a skillet, cook the ground beef until it is no longer pink. Get rid of any excess fat.
- Add the tomato sauce, salt, pepper, and onion powder to the beef and cook on low heat while you finish the remainder of the meal.
- Cook the egg noodles as directed on the packet.
- Combine the sour cream and cottage cheese in a large mixing bowl.
- Drain the noodles and combine them with the sour cream and cottage cheese in a mixing bowl. Toss the noodles in the sauce to evenly coat them.
- Half of the egg noodle mixture must be poured into the prepared pan, followed by half of the ground beef combination and half of the shredded cheese. Repeat this procedure.
- And bake for Twenty minutes.

Nutrition

Calories: 430 | Carbohydrates: 4g | Sugar: 3g | Protein: 30g | Fat: 32g

Saturated Fat: 15g | Cholesterol: 110mg

KETO ZUCCHINI RAVIOLI

Prep Time: 30 Minutes

Cook Time: 30 Minutes

Serves: 6

Baked Zucchini Ravioli is a spicy, cheesy, and low-carb dinner that the whole family will enjoy!

Ingredients

- 1 lb. lean ground beef
- 3 zucchinis
- 1 teaspoon Italian seasoning
- 1 teaspoon onion powder
- 1 cup mozzarella cheese
- 1 ½ cups low carb tomato sauce

- ½ teaspoon garlic powder
- 2 tablespoons cream cheese
- ¼ cup parmesan cheese shredded

Instructions

1. Preheat the oven to 350 degrees Fahrenheit.
2. Cut thin slices of zucchini with a vegetable peeler. Set aside.
3. In a small pan, brown the beef and seasonings, breaking it up as finely as possible. Drain fat.
4. Combine cream cheese and 2 tablespoons of parmesan cheese in a mixing bowl.
5. Make an 'X' shape with two zucchini strips. Fill with 2 tbsp. Meat stuffing. To make a tiny bundle, wrap zucchini around the steak.
6. Spread ½ cup pasta sauce in the bottom of a baking dish. On a serving plate, arrange the zucchini ravioli. Top with the leftover pasta sauce, mozzarella cheese, and parmesan cheese.
7. Bake for twenty-five-thirty minutes, or until bubbling and cooked.

Nutrition

Calories: 226.64 | Carbohydrates: 7.76g | Fiber: 2.09g | Sugar: 5.48g | Protein: 24.2g

Fat: 11.13g | Saturated Fat: 5.87g | Cholesterol: 69.77mg

PROSCIUTTO-WRAPPED CHICKEN WITH MUSHROOM SAUCE

Prep Time: 10 Minutes

Cook Time: 50 Minutes

Serves: 4

With crispy prosciutto and a luscious mushroom sauce, the ordinary chicken meal is transformed.

Ingredients

- 200g small Swiss brown mushrooms, thickly sliced
- 4 small chicken breast fillets
- 2 spring onions, finely chopped
- 150g prosciutto
- 20g butter

- 2 teaspoon honey
- 300ml Bulla Cooking Cream
- 2 tablespoons dry sherry
- 2 cloves garlic, crushed
- 1 tablespoon Dijon mustard
- Sliced roast Brussels sprouts, to serve, optional

Instructions

1. Preheat the oven to 180 degrees Celsius/160 degrees Celsius fan-forced. The nonstick baking paper must be used to line an oven pan. Season each chicken breast with a pinch of black pepper. Top each breast fillet with a sprinkling of spring onions. Wrap the prosciutto around the meat and set it on the prepared tray. Bake for thirty-five to forty minutes, or until chicken is cooked through and prosciutto is lightly crisped. Reserve tray juices
2. Meanwhile, in a large nonstick frying pan, melt butter over medium-low heat. Cook, frequently stirring, for four-five minutes, or until golden brown and melted. If the mushrooms require moisture, add a splash of water. Cook for one minute after adding the garlic.
3. Cook for one minute after adding the sherry. Combine the cream, mustard, and honey in a mixing bowl. Simmer for one-two minutes, or until sauce has thickened somewhat. Simmer for one minute more after adding the reserved pan juices and seasoning well. Remove the pan from the heat. Cut the chicken into thick slices or serve it whole. Serve with crispy roasted Brussel sprouts as a side dish.

Nutrition

Calories: 254 | Fat: 9g | Saturated Fat: 2g | Protein: 39g | Cholesterol: 105mg

Carbohydrates: 3g | Sodium: 458mg

MACADAMIA-CRUSTED FISH WITH HERB SALAD

Prep Time: 15 Minutes

Cook Time: 20 Minutes

Serves: 4

This Macadamia-crusted fish with herb salad is a terrific midweek dish with a dusting of native spice and a large dose of real blue flavor.

Ingredients

- 2 tablespoons extra virgin olive oil
- 2 cups unsalted macadamias
- Grated zest and juice of 1 lemon, plus wedges to serve
- 1 garlic clove, chopped
- 4 x 160g skinless barramundi fillets

- 50g mixed salad leaves, to serve
- 1/2 bunch each flat-leaf parsley and chives

Instructions

1. Preheat the oven to 200°C and line a baking sheet with parchment paper.
2. In a small food processor, whiz the nuts, garlic, zest, half the juice, and 1 tbsp oil into a coarse paste. Season and transfer to a bowl. Finely chop 2 tablespoons each parsley and chives and stir in.
3. Place the fish on the tray and cover with the nut mixture. Bake for fifteen-twenty minutes, or until the fish is opaque and the crust is brown.
4. Remove the remaining parsley leaves and cut the chives in half. Combine salad leaves, remaining oil, and lemon juice in a mixing bowl. Season to taste, then serve with lemon slices and fish.

Nutrition

Calories: 786 | Fat: 69g | Fiber: 5g | Protein: 37g | Sugar: 3g | Carbohydrates: 3g

Cholesterol: 86mg | Sodium: 532.26mg

MAPLE-GLAZED SALMON WITH SPINACH AND BROCCOLINI

Prep Time: 20 Minutes

Cook Time: 15 Minutes

Serves: 4

This Maple Glazed Salmon is sweet, wonderfully seasoned, and full of melt-in-your-mouth taste in every bite! This is the perfect healthy evening dinner, and it only takes a few minutes to prepare!

Ingredients

- 1 tablespoon tamari sauce
- 1 tablespoon maple syrup
- 1 tablespoon wholegrain mustard

- 400g piece skinless salmon, pin-boned
- 1 bunch asparagus, trimmed
- ½ teaspoon each black & white sesame seeds, mixed, plus extra to serve
- 2 tablespoons avocado oil
- Juice of ½ lemon, remaining cut into wedges, to serve
- 1½ cups coriander & mint leaves
- 1 bunch broccolini, trimmed, thicker stems cut in half lengthways
- Mixed salad leaves & sauerkraut -optional

Instructions

1. In a broad, shallow bowl, combine maple syrup, half of the mustard, and half of the tamari sauce. Toss in the salmon and turn to coat. Set aside for fifteen minutes to marinate.
2. Preheat the oven grill to its highest setting. Place the salmon on a baking pan that has been lightly oiled and sprinkled with half of the sesame seeds. In a mixing bowl, combine the asparagus, broccolini, 1/2 tablespoons oil, and the remaining sesame seeds, season to taste, and toss to coat. Arrange veggies on the tray around salmon and cook on the top level for six-eight minutes, turning once, until fish is lightly coated and medium-rare and vegetables are just tender. Allow 5 minutes for the salmon to rest before flaking.
3. Season with salt and pepper and shake the remaining mustard, tamari, and oil with the lemon juice in a small screw-top container to prepare the dressing.
4. On a serving tray, arrange the coriander, mint, salad leaves, broccolini, asparagus, and herbs, then top with the salmon and drizzle with the dressing. Serve With sauerkraut.

Nutrition

Calories: 383 | Fat: 8g | Protein: 25g | Sodium: 450mg | Sugar:6g | Carbohydrates: 2g

LOW CARB MOROCCAN LAMB WITH CARROT

Prep Time: 15 Minutes

Cook Time: 5 Minutes

Serves: 4

Here's a quick and easy Moroccan marinade for lamb that's packed with flavor. The cold flavors of mint, carrots, and Greek-style yogurt complement the barbecued meat well.

Ingredients

- 2 garlic cloves, crushed
- 2 teaspoons dried oregano
- 3 tablespoons olive oil
- 2 teaspoons sweet paprika
- 2 tablespoons sumac
- 12 French-trimmed lamb cutlets
- 2 teaspoons cumin

- 4 carrots, peeled, thinly sliced
- 95g kalamata olives
- 1/4 cup chopped flat-leaf parsley
- 6 radishes, thinly sliced
- 1 tablespoon red wine vinegar
- Greek-style yogurt, to serve
- 2 teaspoons harissa-optional

Instructions

1. Combine garlic, paprika, sumac, oregano, 1 tablespoon oil, and 2 tablespoons of water. Set aside after rubbing the mixture over the cutlets.
2. Carrots should be cooked for two minutes. Cumin, parsley, harissa, remaining oil, vinegar, and 2 tablespoons of water are mixed together. Drain carrots and combine with dressing, olives, and radishes in a large mixing bowl.
3. Grill or barbecue the lamb for two minutes on each side over high heat or until it is just cooked through. Serve with a salad and a smear of yogurt on top.

Nutrition

Calories: 498 | Fat: 35g | Sugar: 4g | Fiber: 6g | Protein: 36g | Carbohydrates: 3g

Cholesterol: 121mg | Sodium: 561.37mg

PLUM AND SMOKED TROUT SCANDI BOWL

Prep Time: 20 Minutes

Cook Time: 20 Minutes

Serves: 4

This superfood Superbowl is light, fresh, and full of healthy ingredients, not to mention delicious!

Ingredients

- 1 cup raw buckwheat, plus 2 tsp extra, toasted
- 1 baby golden or red beetroot, very thinly sliced
- 1 teaspoon caraway seeds, toasted
- Finely grated zest and juice of 1/2 a lemon
- 1/2 cup creme fraiche
- 1 cup loosely packed watercress sprigs

- 2 (480g) whole smoked trout, skin, and bones removed, flaked
- 2 plums, thinly sliced
- 1 baby fennel, very thinly sliced, fronds reserved
- 1 red eschalot, thinly sliced

Instructions

1. In a small bowl, combine creme fraiche, caraway seeds, and lemon zest, and juice.
2. In a saucepan over high heat, combine buckwheat and 1 3/4 cup (430ml) water. Bring to a boil, then reduce to low heat and simmer for eighteen-twenty minutes, covered, until just tender. Drain. Using a fork, stir through 2 tbs creme fraiche mixture
3. Fill serving bowls halfway with buckwheat. Beetroot, plum, fennel, fish, watercress, and eschalot go on top. To serve, drizzle with the remaining crème Fraiche mixture and top with toasted buckwheat and fennel fronds.

Nutrition

Calories: 251 | Fat: 11g | Fiber: 0g | Sugar: 0g | Protein: 35g | Cholesterol: 105mg

Sodium: 607mg | Carbohydrates: 7g

KETO PRAWN TOM YUM

Prep Time: 5 Minutes

Cook Time: 15 Minutes

Serves: 4

This classic Thai cuisine succeeds on all three fronts: fast, simple, and flavorful with a Monday-to-Friday meal idea.

Ingredients

- 1 tablespoon ginger, grated
- 1 lemongrass stalk, bruised
- 2 tablespoons peanut oil
- 1/2 bunch spring onions, white part sliced, green part thinly sliced on an angle
- 2 garlic cloves
- 1/4 cup lime juice
- 2 tablespoons fish sauce

- 2 teaspoons sambal oelek
- 2 kaffir lime leaves
- 2 teaspoons caster sugar
- 200g dried pad Thai rice noodles
- 16 green prawns, peeled, deveined
- 2 cups Massel chicken style liquid stock
- 250g punnet cherry tomatoes, halved Coriander leaves, to serve

Instructions

1. In a large skillet, heat the oil over medium heat. Cook, constantly stirring, for one-two minutes, until garlic, ginger, lemongrass, and white spring onion are fragrant.
2. Cook, constantly stirring, for one minute after adding the sambal oelek, sugar, and kaffir lime leaves, then add the lime juice, fish sauce, stock, and 3 cups water. Bring to a low boil, then reduce to low heat and cook for four to five minutes until the flavors have permeated. Cook for three-four minutes, or until prawns are just cooked, before adding tomatoes and prawns.
3. Meanwhile, prepare the noodles according to the package directions. Finally, drain the water and set it aside.
4. To serve, divide noodles among dishes, ladle soup over them, then garnish with coriander leaves and the leftover spring onion.

Nutrition

Calories: 381 | Net Carbohydrates: 8.4g | Fiber: 3.5g | Sugar: 2g | Protein: 21.5g

Fat: 29g

CHILI-LIME BAKED SALMON IN FOIL

Prep Time: 5 Minutes

Cook Time: 15 Minutes

Serves: 4

The finest foil-baked salmon dish ever! Chipotle chili, brushed with my lime and chile sauce, dusted with a dash of cumin. This recipe is simple to prepare and takes less than thirty minutes to complete. When cooked in foil, the salmon becomes flakey and delicate.

Ingredients

- 2 teaspoons honey
- 1 clove garlic, minced
- 1 ¼ pound sockeye or Coho salmon
- 1/4 teaspoon red pepper flakes
- 2 tablespoons lime juice + 1 teaspoon lime zest

- 1/2 teaspoon chipotle chili powder
- 1/2 teaspoon cumin powder
- 1 tablespoon cilantro, chopped
- 1/2 teaspoon salt
- 2 tablespoons cold butter, cubed

Instructions

1. Preheat the oven to 375 degrees Fahrenheit and place a rack in the center.
2. Combine the lime juice, red pepper flakes, honey, garlic, and salt in a medium saucepan over medium heat. Allow 1 tablespoon of lime juice to reduce.
3. Remove the pan from the heat and swirl in 1 tablespoon of butter to allow the butter to melt. Return to the heat for a few seconds, then remove from the heat and continue to swirl until the butter has totally melted. Replace the second tablespoon of butter and repeat the process. Remove the sauce from the heat once the butter has completely melted.
4. Fill a piece of foil large enough to fold over and seal with the salmon fillet. Brush the lime butter sauce over the fish using a brush or a spoon. Cumin powder, lime zest, and chili powder are used to season. Cover with foil, making sure all sides are properly sealed to prevent the sauce from leaking.
5. Preheat the oven to 350°F and bake the salmon for twelve-fourteen minutes, or until firm. Allow the fish to broil for two to three minutes under the broiler, keeping an eye on it to ensure it does not burn. Remove from the oven and sprinkle with cilantro. Serve right away.

Nutrition

Calories: 274 | Fat: 14.3g | Sugar: 3.1g | Protein: 31g | Cholesterol: 79.1mg

Sodium: 366.3mg | Carbohydrates: 4.1g | Fiber: 0.5g

EASY KETO BAKED ITALIAN SAUSAGE

Prep Time: 5 Minutes

Cook Time: 40 Minutes

Serves: 7

This Easy Keto Baked Italian Sausage Dinner is a tasty and easy meal that you'll want to make again and again. This low-carb, flavor-packed dish has seared sausage slathered in marinara sauce and topped with melted mozzarella cheese.

Ingredients

- 24 or 25.5 oz Low Carb Marinara Sauce
- 1 ½ cup mozzarella cheese
- 2 packs Italian sausage
- ½ cup water
- ½ teaspoon basil seasoning

- ¼ teaspoon garlic powder
- ¼ cup Parmesan Cheese
- ¼ teaspoon Italian seasonings
- ⅛ pepper

Instructions

1. Brown the Italian sausage links on each side in a skillet placed over medium heat.
2. Add 1/2 cup water and cook on low for eight minutes with the cover on.
3. In a greased 9 x 13 casserole dish, place the sausages.
4. Pour 24 ounces of marinara sauce on top.
5. Sprinkle 1 ½ cup shredded mozzarella cheese and ¼ cup Parmesan cheese over top of your sausages.
6. Season the cheeses with salt and pepper.
7. Bake for eighteen minutes at 375°F, then move to the top rack of the oven for the final 2 minutes. Turn the oven to broil for the last minute if you want the cheese to be extra bubbly and browned, but keep an eye on it!

Nutrition

Calories: 480 | Carbohydrates: 9g | Fiber: 2g | Sugar: 3g | Protein: 8g

Fat: 26g | Cholesterol: 107mg

KETO COD PICCATA

Prep Time: 5 Minutes

Cook Time: 10 Minutes

Serves: 4

Cod Piccata is a delectable seafood version of the classic piccata. Cod fillets are dredged in flour and pan-fried. Piccata sauce is a tangy, lemony butter sauce that goes nicely with the fish. This light, healthful dinner is quick and easy to prepare, making it ideal for hectic weeknights.

Ingredients

<u>Cod Fish</u>

- 1 tablespoon extra-virgin olive oil
- 1/2 cup blanched almond flour
- 1 tablespoon unsalted butter
- 1.5 pounds cod fish fillets
- 1/2 teaspoon salt

- 1/4 teaspoon pepper

Piccata Sauce

- 1 tablespoon unsalted butter
- 1/4 cup fresh squeezed lemon juice
- 1 shallot
- 4 cloves garlic minced
- 1/4 cup capers
- 1 cup white wine
- fresh parsley (optional, garnish)

Instructions

Cod Fish

1. On a plate, combine the almond flour, salt, and pepper. Place the cod on a plate after dredging it in the flour mixture.
2. In a large skillet, melt the butter and olive oil over medium-high heat. Add the fish once the butter-oil mixture is heated and sizzles when water is splashed over it. Cook for two-three minutes until golden brown, then flip and cook for another 2 minutes, or until the salmon is opaque throughout and flakes readily with a fork. Place on a clean plate.

Piccata Sauce

1. Reduce the heat to medium-low and stir in the remaining butter. Once the butter has melted, add the shallots and garlic and simmer for two minutes, or until softened.
2. Pour in the wine gradually, increase the heat, and bring to a boil. Scrape up any browned bits as you reduce by half. Stir in the lemon juice and capers.
3. Return the fish to the pan to finish cooking.
4. If desired, serve the fish with spoonful of piccata sauce on top and fresh parsley on the side.

Nutrition

Calories: 364 | Carbohydrates: 8g | Fiber: 2g | Sugar: 2g | Protein: 34g

Fat: 17g | Saturated Fat: 5g | Cholesterol: 88mg

KETO BLACKENED HALIBUT

Prep Time: 5 Minutes

Cook Time: 15 Minutes

Serves: 4

Blackened Halibut is a quick and easy dish that's ideal for hectic weeknights. This spicy, smoky seafood dish takes only 15 minutes to prepare and only a few ingredients. The Avocado Lime Crema balances out the heat and adds a little zing to the dish.

Ingredients

Blackened Halibut

- 2 tablespoons blackening seasoning
- 1 1/2 pounds halibut fillets
- 1 tablespoon avocado oil

Avocado Lime Crema

- 1/2 cup sour cream
- 1 lime juiced
- 1/2 cup fresh cilantro
- 1 avocado
- pinch salt

Instructions

Blackened Halibut

1. Apply the blackening seasoning to both sides of the halibut fillets and press it into the fish.
2. In a large skillet, heat the oil over medium heat.
3. When the pan is hot, add the fillets and cook for three-five minutes per side, or until the seasoning is scorched and the fish is opaque and easily flaked. Then, using a meat thermometer inserted into the thickest section, it should attain an internal temperature of 145°F.

Avocado Lime Crema

1. In a blender cup or food processor, combine the avocado flesh, lime juice, sour cream, cilantro, and salt to produce the Avocado Lime Crema. Taste and adjust seasoning if necessary, after blending until smooth and creamy.
2. Serve the fillets with a dollop of avocado sauce on top.

Nutrition

Calories: 323 | Carbohydrates: 6g | Fiber: 3g | Sugar: 1g | Protein: 33g

Fat: 19g | Cholesterol: 98mg

KETO CHICKEN FLORENTINE

Prep Time: 10 Minutes

Cook Time: 20 Minutes

Serves: 4

Keto Chicken Florentine is a one-pan meal recipe that is simple to prepare. This low-carb chicken skillet dinner features seared chicken breasts and a delicious, creamy spinach sauce.

Ingredients

Chicken

- 1-pound boneless, skinless chicken breasts
- 1 tablespoon butter
- 1/2 teaspoon salt
- 1/4 teaspoon pepper

Creamy Spinach Sauce

- 1 shallot finely diced
- 4 cloves garlic minced
- 1 1/2 cups white wine
- 1/2 cup Parmesan cheese
- 2 tablespoons butter
- 1 cup heavy whipping cream
- 5 ounces fresh spinach
- fresh parsley -optional

Instructions

Chicken

1. Using salt and pepper, season the chicken. To use the almond flour, cover both sides of each piece.
2. In a large skillet over medium-high heat, melt 1 tablespoon of butter. Cook until golden brown and cooked through, about two-three minutes per side. A meat thermometer inserted into the thickest area of the chicken will indicate 165°F internal temperature. Transfer to a plate that has been cleaned.

Creamy Spinach Sauce

1. Return the pan to a medium heat level on the burner. Combine the 2 tablespoons butter, shallot, and garlic in a mixing bowl. Cook for two-three minutes, or until the vegetables are softened.
2. Increase the heat and add the wine. Scrape up any browned parts from the bottom of the pan and reduce them by half. Stir in the heavy cream once the sauce has reduced. Cook for a few minutes to thicken the sauce.
3. Cook until the spinach is wilted, about two-three minutes in the skillet.
4. Return the chicken pieces to the pan to reheat.
5. Using a spoon, drizzle the sauce over the chicken. If using, top with Parmesan cheese and parsley. Serve right away.

Nutrition

Calories: 550 | Carbohydrates: 8g | Fiber: 1g | Sugar: 2g | Protein: 31g

Fat: 37g | Cholesterol: 185mg

KETO CAJUN SHRIMP AND GRITS

Prep Time: 15 Minutes

Cook Time: 20 Minutes

Serves: 4

The original southern comfort food classic, Keto Cajun Shrimp and Grits, is a low-carb recipe based on the original southern comfort food classic. Buttery, cheesy cauliflower grits are topped with spicy shrimp and bacon. This dish is every bit as delicious as the original

Ingredients

<u>Cheesy Cauliflower Grits</u>

- 1 cup heavy cream
- 1 large head cauliflower
- 1 tablespoon unsalted butter
- 1 cup sharp cheddar cheese

- 1/2 teaspoon salt
- 1/4 teaspoon pepper

Cajun Shrimp

- 1-pound large shrimp - peeled and deveined
- 1 tablespoon Cajun seasoning
- 4 cloves garlic minced
- 5 slices bacon diced
- lemon wedges

Instructions

1. In a large saucepan, combine the cauliflower, salt, pepper, heavy cream, and butter and bring to a simmer over medium-high heat. It's best if the mixture is pretty thick.
2. Cook, frequently stirring, for about ten minutes or until the cauliflower is soft. Remove the pan from the heat and add the cheese.
3. Add the bacon to a large skillet over medium heat and cook, stirring regularly, until crisp, about ten minutes while the grits are cooking. With a slotted spoon, transfer the bacon to a paper towel-lined dish.
4. Return the pan to the stovetop after draining all except 1 tablespoon of the fat. Toss the shrimp with the Cajun spice before placing them in a single layer in the pan. Cook for one-two minutes without stirring, then flip and cook for another one-two minutes, or until opaque.
5. Return the garlic and bacon to the pan and stir to mix during the last thirty-sixty seconds of cooking.
6. Toss the grits with the shrimp and bacon mixture before serving. If desired, squeeze lemon juice over the top.

Nutrition

Calories: 635 | Carbohydrates: 6g | Fiber: 5g | Sugar: 4g | Protein: 39g

Fat: 48g | Cholesterol: 423mg

HERBED GORGONZOLA STEAK BUTTER

Prep Time: 10 Minutes

Cook Time: 20 Minutes

Serves: 4

Give your steak a little extra richness and bite with a pat of this delicious Herbed Gorgonzola Steak Butter. It's a simple compound butter that adds even more taste to a properly cooked steak.

Ingredients

- 1 clove garlic - minced
- 1 teaspoon fresh parsley - minced
- 4 tablespoons Gorgonzola cheese
- 4 tablespoons unsalted butter at room temperature

Instructions

1. In a small bowl, combine the butter, Gorgonzola cheese, garlic, and parsley. Toss with a fork until everything is well combined.
2. Refrigerate until ready to use.
3. Place the pats of butter on a plate or in a bowl.
4. Cook for ten-twenty minutes, depending on the thickness of the streaks.
5. Plate your steaks when they've finished grilling and top them with a dollop of Gorgonzola butter while they're still hot. Allow the butter to melt before eating.

Nutrition

Calories: 75 | Saturated Fat: 4g | Protein: 1g | Fat: 7g | Cholesterol: 20mg

Sodium: 98mg

GARLIC BUTTER STEAK BITES WITH CAULIFLOWER

Prep Time: 10 Minutes

Cook Time: 25 Minutes

Serves: 4

Dinner can't go wrong with a thick, buttery steak, especially when it's so delectable and easy to make. Garlic Butter Steak Bites are served with a side of cauliflower to keep the meal modest in calories and carbohydrates.

Ingredients

- 4 tablespoons butter
- 1 head cauliflower
- 2 pounds steak 1 teaspoon salt
- 1/2 teaspoon pepper
- 1 tablespoon fresh thyme
- 6 cloves garlic - minced

Instructions

1. Season the pieces of steak with 1/2 teaspoon of salt and 1/4 teaspoon of pepper.
2. Melt 1 tablespoon of the butter over medium-high heat in a large, deep skillet or cast-iron pan,
3. Cook until the steak is browned on all sides and cooked through. Transfer to a plate.
4. Cook, frequently tossing, until the florets are barely fork-tender, about 7-10 minutes depending on their size. Place on a plate.
5. In the same hot pan, add the remaining 2 tablespoons of butter.
6. Combine the minced garlic and thyme in a mixing bowl.
7. Cook for another minute, then add the meat and cauliflower back in.
8. If preferred, top with additional fresh thyme.

Nutrition

Calories: 617 | Carbohydrates: 9g | Fiber: 3g | Sugar: 3g | Protein: 49g

Fat: 44g | Cholesterol: 168mg

CHEESY BUFFALO CAULIFLOWER DISH

Prep Time: 10 Minutes

Cook Time: 10 Minutes

Serves: 4

Cheesy Buffalo Cauliflower Bites are topped with melted sharp cheddar cheese and a spicy Buffalo sauce. This simple dish can be served as supper.

Ingredients

- 1 tablespoon extra virgin olive oil
- 4 cups cauliflower florets
- 1/2 cup sharp cheddar cheese
- 1/3 cup Buffalo sauce
- 1/2 teaspoon salt
- 1/4 teaspoon pepper

Instructions

1. Season the cauliflower with salt and pepper after tossing it with olive oil.
2. Place the cauliflower in a single layer in the air fryer basket.
3. Cook for nine minutes, shaking the basket halfway through to ensure even cooking.
4. Remove the cauliflower and combine it with the Buffalo sauce in a mixing bowl.
5. Return the cauliflower to the air fryer basket and sprinkle it with the cheese.
6. Return the basket to the air fryer and cook for another one to two minutes until the cheese has melted.
7. Serve the cauliflower on a dish with Ranch dressing on the side, if preferred.

Nutrition

Calories: 171 | Carbohydrates: 5g | Fiber: 2g | Sugar: 2g | Protein: 9g

Fat: 13g | Cholesterol: 30mg

TURKEY CUTLETS WITH ROSEMARY AND THYME

Prep Time: 5 Minutes

Cook Time: 10 Minutes

Serves: 4

In just 15 minutes, you can have these easy Turkey Cutlets with Rosemary and Thyme on the table. So, all year long, enjoy this delicious weeknight turkey supper!

Ingredients

- 1 tablespoon extra virgin olive oil
- 1 tablespoon rosemary
- 1-pound turkey cutlets
- 1 tablespoon thyme
- 1/2 teaspoon salt
- 1/4 teaspoon ground black pepper

Instructions

1. Clean the turkey cutlets by rinsing them and patting them dry with paper towels.
2. Half of the salt, pepper, rosemary, and thyme must be sprinkled over the cutlets' tops.
3. In a large skillet, heat the olive oil over medium heat.
4. Place the turkey cutlets in the pan, seasoned side down, once the oil is hot. Cover with a lid and season the opposite side of the turkey with the remaining ingredients.
5. Cook for five-six minutes on the first side, or until golden brown.
6. Cook a further three-four minutes, or until the turkey is cooked through, on the other side.

Nutrition

Calories: 148 | Carbohydrates: 1g | Fiber: 1g | Sugar: 1g | Protein: 24g

Fat: 5g | Cholesterol: 61mg

KETO PUMPKIN CHILI

Prep Time: 5 Minutes

Cook Time: 25 Minutes

Serves: 8

Pumpkin Chili is a hearty and delicious mash-up of two of fall's most soothing cuisines! This chili has a distinct, autumnal flavor that is ideal for keeping warm on a chilly autumn day.

Ingredients

- 2 pounds ground beef
- 1 tablespoon extra virgin olive oil
- 1/4 cup shallot
- 4 cloves garlic minced
- 1/2 teaspoon salt
- 1/4 teaspoon pepper

- 1 14.5 ounces can fire-roasted diced tomatoes
- 1 15.5 ounces can black beans, drained
- 2 15-ounce cans of pumpkin puree
- 1 cup beef bone broth
- 3 tablespoons chili powder
- 1 tablespoon ground cumin
- 2 tablespoons adobo sauce

Instructions

1. In a Dutch oven or big soup pot, heat the olive oil over medium-high heat.
2. Cook for two-three minutes, or until the shallots are barely softened, before adding the garlic and shallots.
3. Season the ground beef with salt and pepper, then add the chili powder and cumin to the pot.
4. Cook, occasionally stirring, until the meat is no longer pink, about five-seven minutes.
5. Reduce the heat to medium and add the pumpkin puree, diced tomatoes, black bean, beef stock, and adobo sauce, stirring constantly.
6. Cook until thoroughly heated, then reduce to low heat and cook for at least another ten minutes.

Nutrition

Calories: 432 | Carbohydrates: 14g | Fiber: 8g | Sugar: 5g | Protein: 26g

Fat: 26g | Cholesterol: 81mg

KETO CAJUN JAMBALAYA

Prep Time: 15 Minutes

Cook Time: 25 Minutes

Serves: 6

This Keto Cajun Jambalaya combines Andouille sausage, chicken, shrimp, and vegetables in a rich, creamy Cajun flavored sauce. For a low-carb, gluten-free meal, serve this over cauliflower rice.

Ingredients

- 12 ounces chicken
- 12 ounces Andouille sausage - cut into slices
- 1 tablespoon extra virgin olive oil
- 3 teaspoons Cajun seasoning
- 12 ounces shrimp

- 3 sweet peppers
- 1 sweet onion
- 2 ounces heavy cream
- 2 cloves garlic minced
- cauliflower rice

Instructions

1. In a large skillet, heat the olive oil over medium-high heat.
2. In a skillet, season the shrimp with 1 teaspoon of the Cajun seasoning.
3. Cook for three-four minutes or until the shrimp are opaque, then transfer to a dish.
4. In the same skillet, combine the chicken, sausage, and 1 teaspoon of Cajun seasoning.
5. Cook for five-seven minutes, or until the chicken is no longer pink in the center, then transfer to a plate with the shrimp.
6. Reduce the heat to medium and, if necessary, add a drizzle of oil.
7. Cook for thirty seconds or until the garlic is aromatic.
8. Combine the peppers, onions, and the remaining teaspoon of Cajun seasoning in a mixing bowl.
9. Cook for five-seven minutes, or until the peppers and onions are tender.
10. Cook, constantly stirring, until the cream has thickened, about 0ne-two minutes.
11. Return the shrimp, chicken, and sausage to the pan and cook for one to two minutes until heated through. Serve with cauliflower rice.

Nutrition

Calories: 401 | Carbohydrates: 9g | Fiber: 2g | Sugar: 5g | Protein: 29g

Fat: 27g | Cholesterol: 224mg

GARLIC BUTTER INSTANT POT SHORT RIBS

Prep Time: 20 Minutes

Cook Time: 50 Minutes

Serves: 2

Short ribs with butter, garlic, and fresh thyme are seasoned with a simple mixture of butter, garlic, and fresh thyme in the Instant Pot. In a fraction of the time, you may now experience fall-apart delicious short ribs!

Ingredients

- 1-pound boneless beef short ribs
- 2.5 cups beef bone broth
- 1 tablespoon unsalted butter
- 1 tablespoon fresh thyme
- 3 cloves garlic minced

- 1/2 teaspoon salt
- 1/4 teaspoon pepper

Instructions

1. Trim the short ribs of any excess fat and blot them dry using a paper towel. Salt & pepper to taste. Set aside.
2. Set your Instant Pot to sauté mode. Add the butter and allow it to melt after the screen shows "HOT."
3. Then add the short ribs and sear on the first side until browned. It will take roughly seven-eight minutes to complete this task. Then flip the short ribs and sear for three-four minutes on the other side. Finally, remove the ribs from the pan and place them on a dish.
4. In the Instant Pot, combine the garlic and thyme. Cook for one minute, then add a splash of bone broth to deglaze the bottom of the pot, scraping any chunks off the bottom with a wooden or silicone spoon.
5. Remove the ribs from the saucepan and turn off the sauté function. Pour in enough bone broth to slightly cover the ribs. Depending on the size of your short ribs and the Instant Pot you're using, you may require more or less than the recipe specifies.
6. Make sure the valve on the instant pot is in the seal position before putting the lid on. Set the pressure cooker on high for thirty-five minutes, followed by a fifteen-minute natural release.
7. After the natural release time has passed, carefully open the pot and turn the valve to vent.
8. Optionally, you may use your Instant Pot to make soup and decrease the residual liquid by half by bringing it to a boil. It may take up to thirty minutes to complete this task. However, because the broth is likely to be salty, a modest amount will go a long way!
9. Top these Garlic Butter Instant Pot Short Ribs with leftover sauce from the pot and fresh thyme before serving.

Nutrition

Calories: 490 | Carbohydrates: 1g | Saturated Fat: 13g | Protein: 54g

Fat: 28g | Cholesterol: 148mg

CREAMY TUSCAN CHICKEN

Prep Time: 5 Minutes

Cook Time: 35 Minutes

Serves: 4

This delectable Tuscan-style chicken meal is prepared with vegetables for simplicity of cooking and olives for juicy tartness. This is a keto-friendly dish.

Ingredients

- 4 boneless skinless chicken breasts
- 3 tablespoons butter
- 3 cloves garlic, minced
- 1 tablespoon extra-virgin olive oil
- Kosher salt
- Freshly ground black pepper

- 1 teaspoon dried oregano
- 1/4 cup freshly grated Parmesan
- 1 1/2 cup cherry tomatoes, halved
- 3 cup baby spinach
- 1/2 cup heavy cream
- Lemon wedges, for serving

Instructions

1. Heat the oil in a pan over medium heat. Season the chicken with salt, pepper, and oregano. Cook for eight minutes per side, or until golden and no longer pink. Remove the pan from the heat and set it aside.
2. Melt butter in the same skillet over medium heat. Stir in the garlic and simmer for one minute or until fragrant. Season with salt and pepper and add cherry tomatoes. Heat until the tomatoes begin to burst, then add the spinach and cook until it begins to wilt.
3. Bring the mixture to a boil with heavy cream and parmesan cheese. Reduce heat to low and cook for three minutes, or until sauce is slightly condensed. Return the chicken to the skillet and cook for another five to seven minutes, or until well cooked.
4. Serve with lemon slices on the side.

Nutrition

Calories: 380 | Protein: 29g | Fiber: 5g | Sugar: 2g | Carbohydrates: 28g

Fat: 1g | Saturated Fat: 14g

LEMON SOY ROASTED BRANZINO

Prep Time: 10 Minutes

Cook Time: 15 Minutes

Serves: 4

This Lemon Soy Roasted Branzino is a unique take on a classic meal, and it's the greatest non-Chinese fish you've ever had. It doesn't have many bothersome small bones, and it's rather simple to handle and prepare.

Ingredients

- 2 tablespoons soy sauce
- 4 tablespoons melted butter
- 3 16 oz. whole branzino
- juice and zest of ½ a lemon
- 1 tablespoon parsley chopped

- 3 tablespoons extra virgin olive oil
- 3 sprigs thyme
- Salt

Instructions

1. Preheat oven to 425 degrees Fahrenheit. Combine the butter, soy sauce, 1/2 lemon juice/zest, and 1 tablespoon minced parsley in a mixing bowl.
2. Season the branzino cavities with salt and pepper, then load each with three lemon rounds and a sprig of thyme.
3. Heat the olive oil in a large nonstick ovenproof skillet until it shimmers. Cook the branzino over high heat for two minutes per side or until the skin is browned and crisp. You may have to perform this in batches.
4. Place the fish on a big baking sheet with a rim. Roast for 9 minutes after drizzling with the butter mixture and seasoning with salt to taste. Finish with one-two minutes under the broiler. To avoid burning, keep an eye on it.
5. Serve with extra chopped parsley as a garnish.

Nutrition

Calories: 353 | Carbohydrates: 1g | Fiber: 1g | Sugar: 1g | Protein: 41g

Fat: 20g | Cholesterol: 202mg